I then bequeath the whole of my property . . . to the United States of America, to found at Washington, under the name of the Smithsonian Institution, an establishment for the increase and diffusion of knowledge among men.

—JAMES SMITHSON

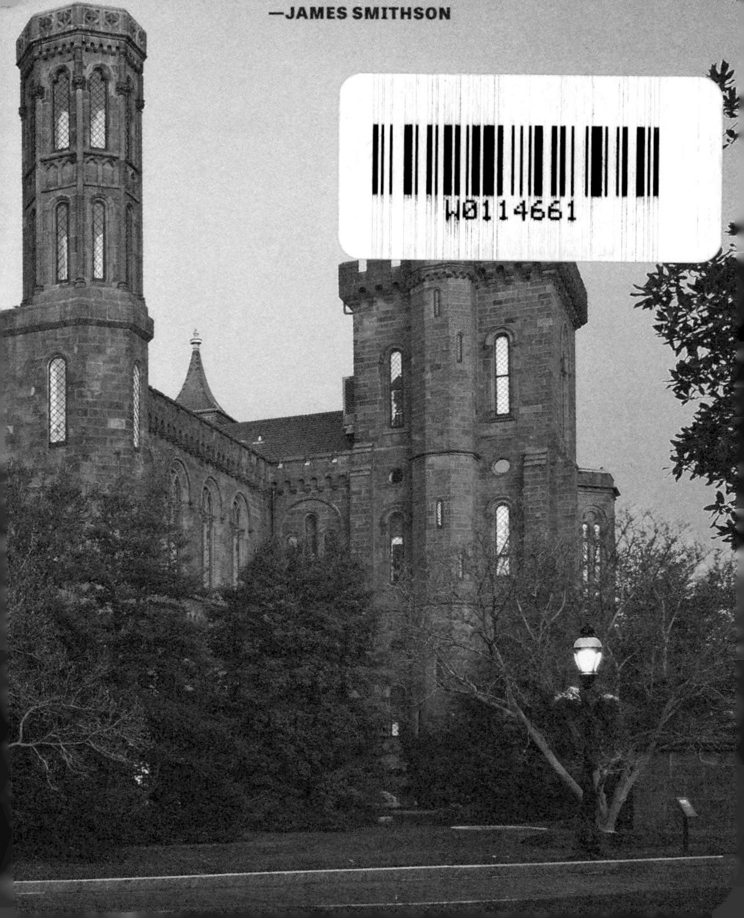

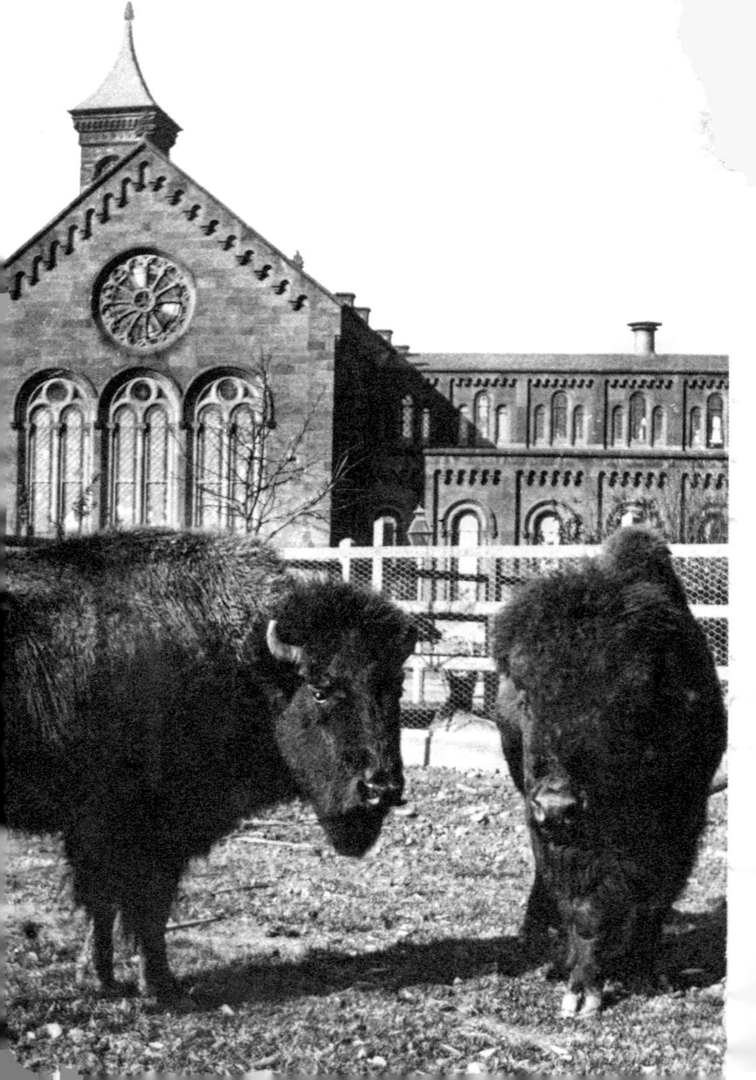

Smithsonian

JOURNAL

SMITHSONIAN BOOKS
WASHINGTON, DC

Published by Smithsonian Books
DIRECTOR: Carolyn Gleason
SENIOR EDITOR: Jaime Schwender
EDITOR: Julie Huggins

DESIGNED BY Joe Newton

This book may be purchased for educational, business, or
sales promotional use. For information, please write:
Special Markets Department, Smithsonian Books, P.O. Box
37012, MRC 513, Washington, DC 20013

Printed in Malaysia, not at government expense
26 25   2 3 4 5

ADD
YOUR
STORY
TO
OURS

As a cultural institution with collections that range widely, from abstract art to zoological specimens, the Smithsonian supports creative and daring endeavors—whether it's painting a monumental portrait of George Washington, like artist Gilbert Stuart, or becoming the first woman to fly solo across the Atlantic Ocean, like aviator Amelia Earhart. Our many museums feature fine arts and crafts from the United States and around the world; the realms of air travel and space flight; the story of our planet; Native American, American, African American, Latino, and Asian history and culture; contemporary design; and postal history and stamps. Our zoo is home to hundreds of species, our libraries house millions of volumes, and our colorful gardens showcase an extraordinary range of seasonal plants. And these diverse ventures often started as ideas, doodles, or random notes on lined journal pages, such as the ones in this book.

Writers often credit their journals with keeping them grounded and helping them reveal inner truths, sparking creativity, and finding inspiration. In a journal, there are no rules. The journal is yours and yours alone. There are no expectations and no mistakes. A journal is also a place to record your memories and preserve how you felt at a particular moment in time. It is a place to truly be yourself. As humorist David Sedaris remarked, "I guess in my diary I'm not afraid to be boring." Writer Anaïs Nin explained the freedom and spontaneity she felt when keeping a journal: "I only wrote of what interested me genuinely, what I felt most strongly at the moment, and I found this fervor, this enthusiasm produced a vividness which often withered in the formal work."

This *Smithsonian Journal* offers the space to scribble, sketch, jot, document, and explore your hopes and dreams. If you need a bit of inspiration, look no further than the quotations printed within. Wisdom from the likes of scientist Albert Einstein, spiritual leader and activist Mahatma Gandhi, former First Lady Michelle Obama, Godfather of Go-Go Chuck

Brown, President Abraham Lincoln, and glass artist Preston Singletary might spur you to reflect on the world around you in a new way.

This intimate book also serves as a wonderful keepsake, with images of historic objects from each of the Smithsonian museums—including the Star-Spangled Banner, the Space Shuttle *Discovery*, Muhammad Ali's boxing gloves, a *Tyrannosurus rex* skeleton—and contemporary works, such as a hand-coiled pot by Kenyan-born artist Magdalene Anyango Namakhiya Odundo, a massive steel sculpture by Mark di Suvero, a black-and-white print of the Manhattan Bridge by photographer Berenice Abbott, and a powwow dress worn to the 2013 inaugural parade by US Army veteran Mitchelene BigMan.

So, follow poet William Wordsworth's sage advice and "fill your paper with the breathings of your heart." Use this elegant book to document travels or stow it under your pillow to preserve dreams. Make lists of your favorite meals or confess your deepest fears. The Smithsonian safeguards the narratives of so many accomplished individuals. Here is a place to tell your own special story and add your personal history to ours.

—by Amy Pastan

The original Star-Spangled Banner flew over Fort McHenry
in 1814 and inspired the words of our National Anthem.
NATIONAL MUSEUM of AMERICAN HISTORY

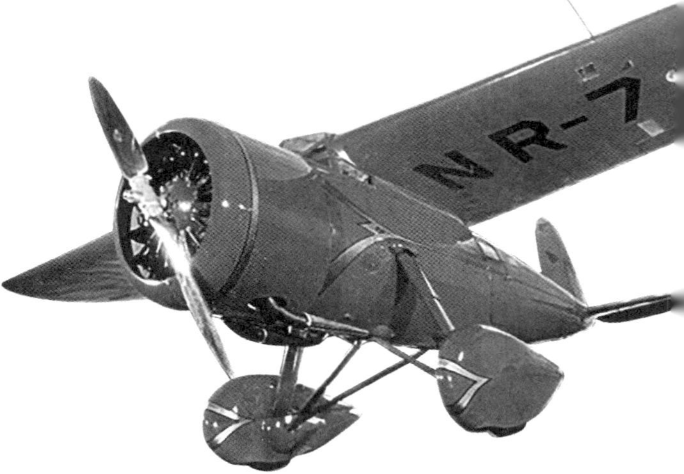
NR-7

Amelia Earhart set two aviation records in this Lockheed 5B Vega. In 1932 she flew it alone across the Atlantic Ocean, then flew it nonstop across the United States—both firsts for a woman.
NATIONAL AIR and SPACE MUSEUM

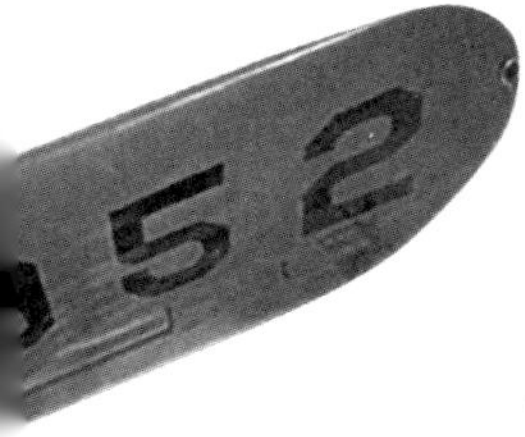
52

THE MOST
DIFFICULT THING IS

THE DECISION TO ACT.

The rest is merely tenacity.

Amelia Earhart

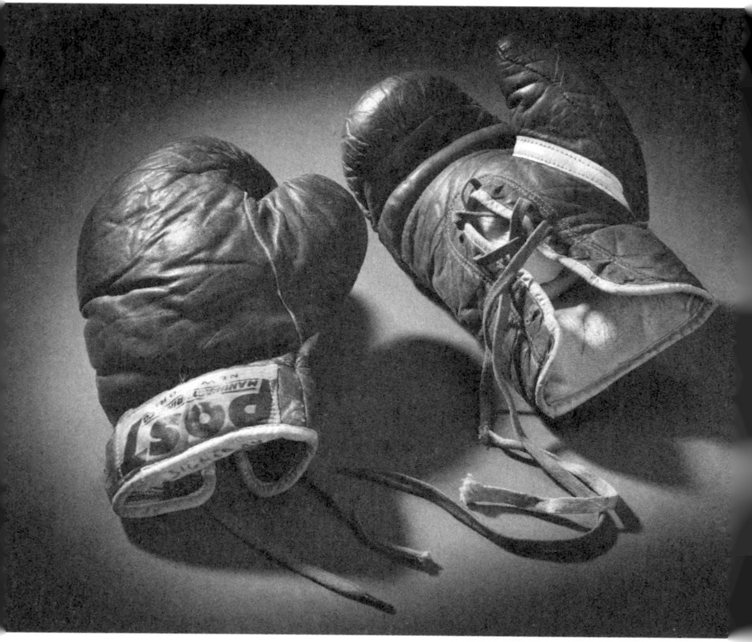

These training boxing gloves were worn and signed by Muhammad Ali in Louisville, Kentucky, in 1960. After winning his first pro fight on October 29, 1960, Ali went on to become a world-renown boxer and political activist.

NATIONAL MUSEUM of AFRICAN AMERICAN HISTORY and CULTURE

Don't count the days;
MAKE
THE DAYS
COUNT.

★ ★ ★ ★ ★

Muhammad Ali

WISDOM

*is not
a product
of schooling
but of the*
LIFELONG
ATTEMPT
to
ACQUIRE IT.

Albert Einstein, 1954

FOR THE INCREASE AND DIFFUSION OF
KNOWLEDGE AMONG MEN

1846 · SMITHSONIAN INSTITUTION · 1946

3¢ UNITED STATES POSTAGE

In 1946, the United States Post Office Department issued this
stamp featuring the Smithsonian Castle to commemorate the
centennial of the Smithsonian Institution, which President
James K. Polk established on August 10, 1846.

NATIONAL POSTAL MUSEUM

Berenice Abbott's striking black-and-white photograph of the Manhattan Bridge in 1936 was part of a decade-long project called *Changing New York* that documented how the city had changed and grown in the 1920s and '30s.
SMITHSONIAN AMERICAN ART MUSEUM

PHOTOGRAPHY DOESN'T TEACH YOU HOW TO EXPRESS YOUR EMOTIONS;

it teaches you

HOW

TO SEE.

✖

Berenice Abbott, 1981

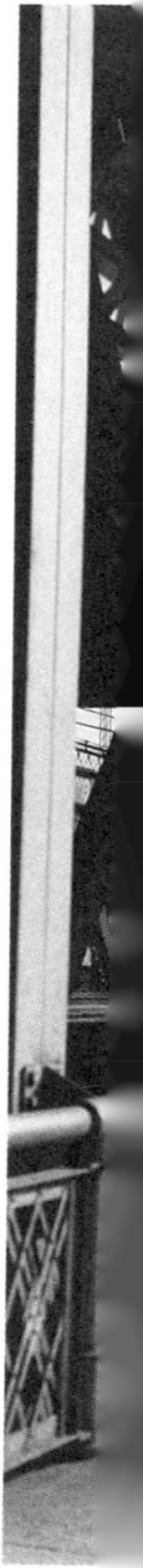

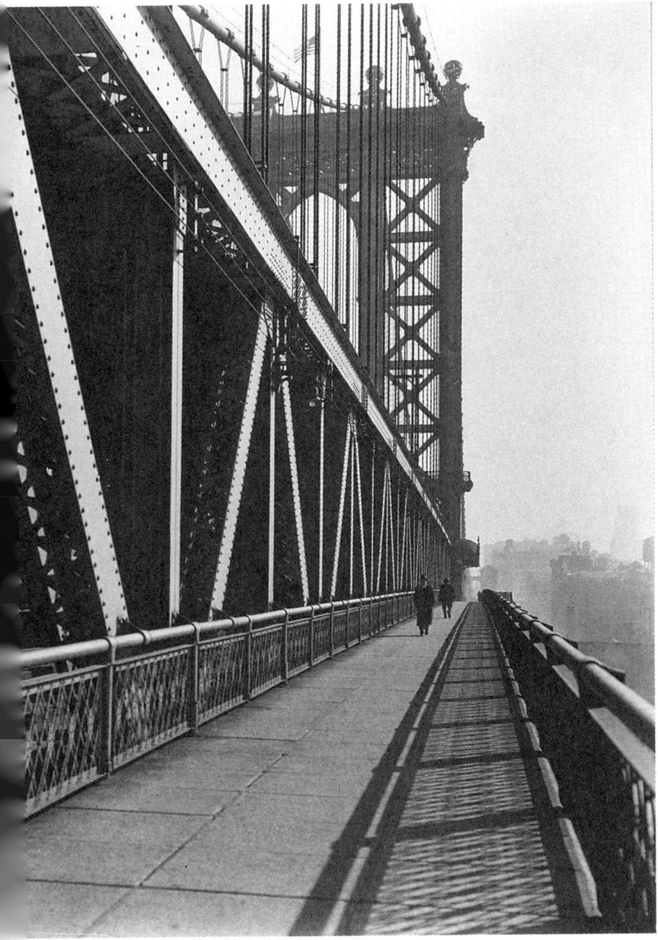

THE WAY TO RIGHT WRONGS

IS TO

TURN

the

LIGHT

of TRUTH

UPON

THEM.

✳

Ida B. Wells, 1892

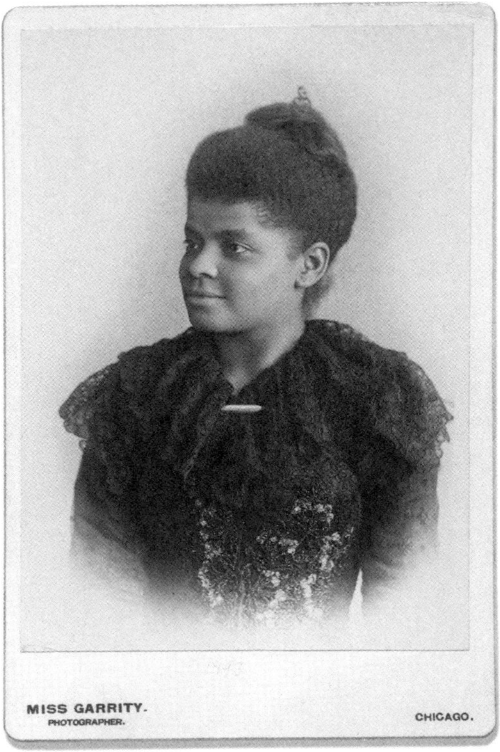
MISS GARRITY.
PHOTOGRAPHER.
CHICAGO.

Investigative journalist, educator, and civil rights activist Ida B. Wells, shown here in a ca. 1893 photograph by Sallie E. Garrity, helped found the National Association for the Advancement of Colored People.
NATIONAL PORTRAIT GALLERY

I BELIEVE THAT

the MAKING
of OBJECTS
TRANSCENDS
BOUNDARIES.

They inform us
of human beings,
rather than the
territory in which
they are located.

Magdalene Odundo, 2019

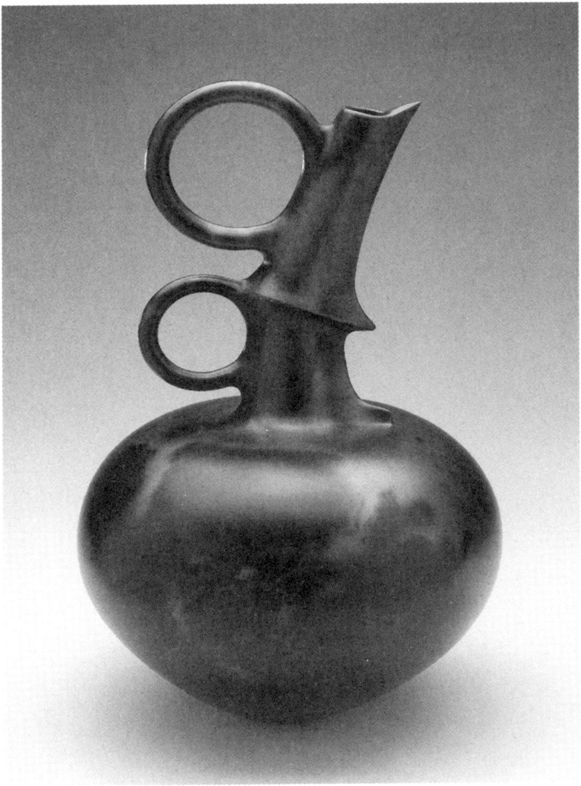

Kenyan-born artist Magdalene Anyango Namakhiya Odundo hand-coiled *Reduced Angled Spouted Black Piece* in 1990, filling the clay gourd-shaped vessel with wood chips and firing it twice to bring out the dark color.

NATIONAL MUSEUM of AFRICAN ART

This sleek 1937 Model 302 telephone, made of cast and enamel-coated metal with a rubber-sheathed cord, was designed by George R. Lum for use throughout the AT&T phone system.
COOPER HEWITT, SMITHSONIAN DESIGN MUSEUM

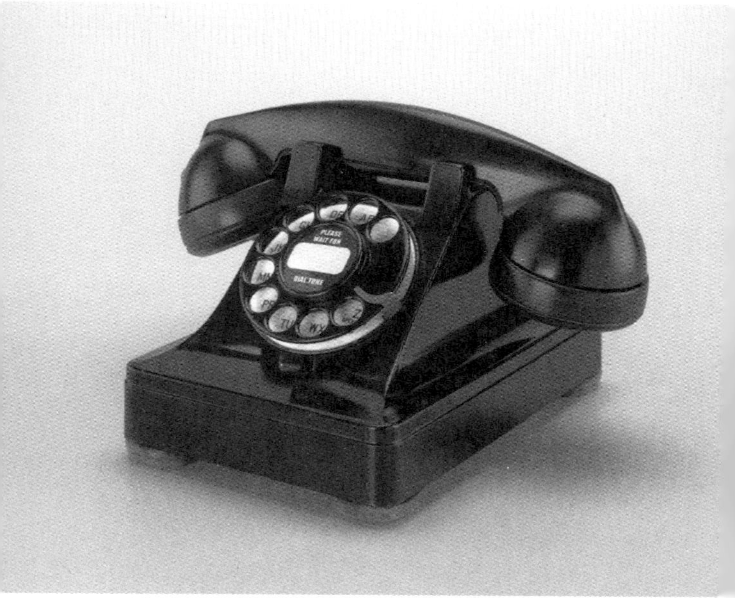
PLEASE WAIT FOR
DIAL TONE

CREATIVITY IS SEEING WHAT
EVERYONE ELSE SEES, BUT THEN

thinking a new thought that has never been thought before and expressing it somehow.

★

Neil DeGrasse Tyson, 2009

I DON'T MEASURE MYSELF BY OTHERS' EXPECTATIONS

or let others define my worth.

Sonia Sotomayor, 2013

Mark di Suvero's massive steel and paint sculpture, *Are Years What? (for Marianne Moore)*, is named after Marianne Moore's poem, "What Are Years?"
HIRSHHORN MUSEUM and SCULPTURE GARDEN

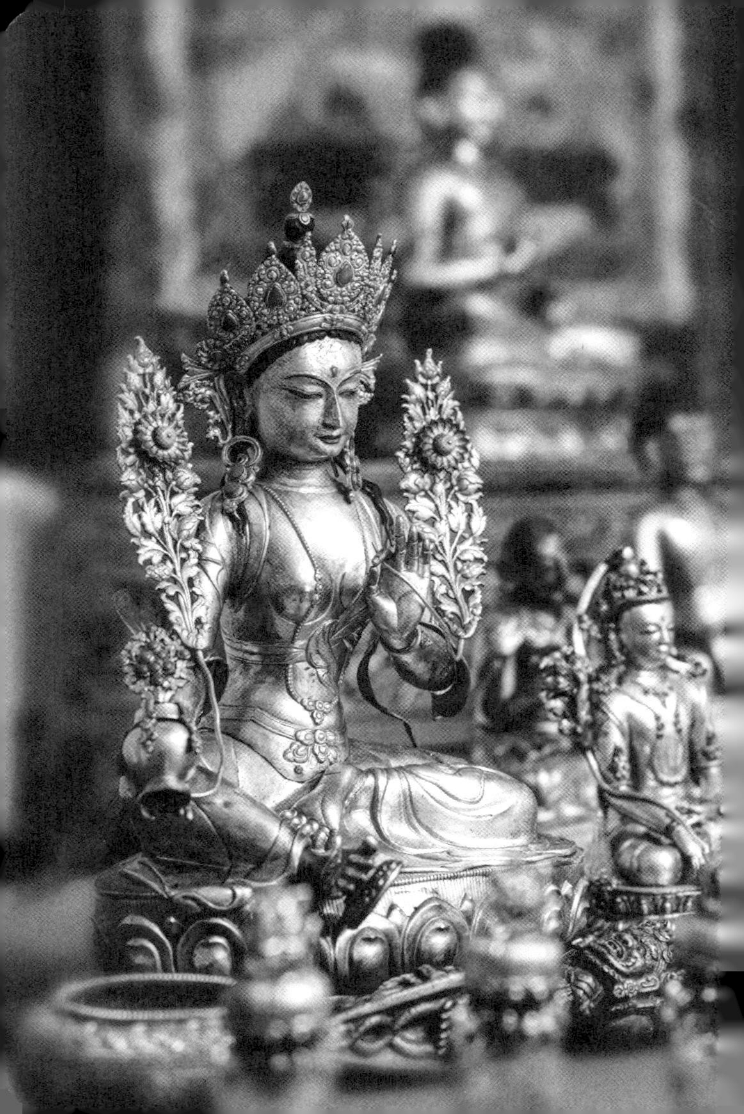

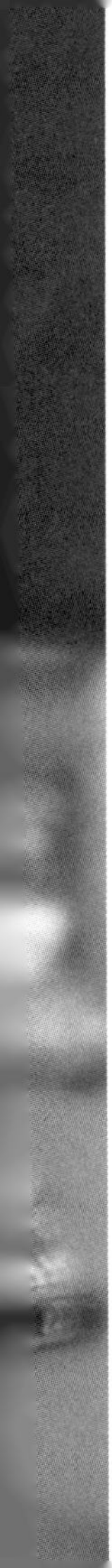

My true religion is Kindness.

**Tenzin Gyatso,
14th Dalai Lama,
1984**

The Tibetan Buddhist Shrine Room uses flickering lights and recorded chanting from Tibetan monks to provide an immersive experience for visitors as they examine its more than 200 objects and artworks.
ARTHUR M. SACKLER GALLERY

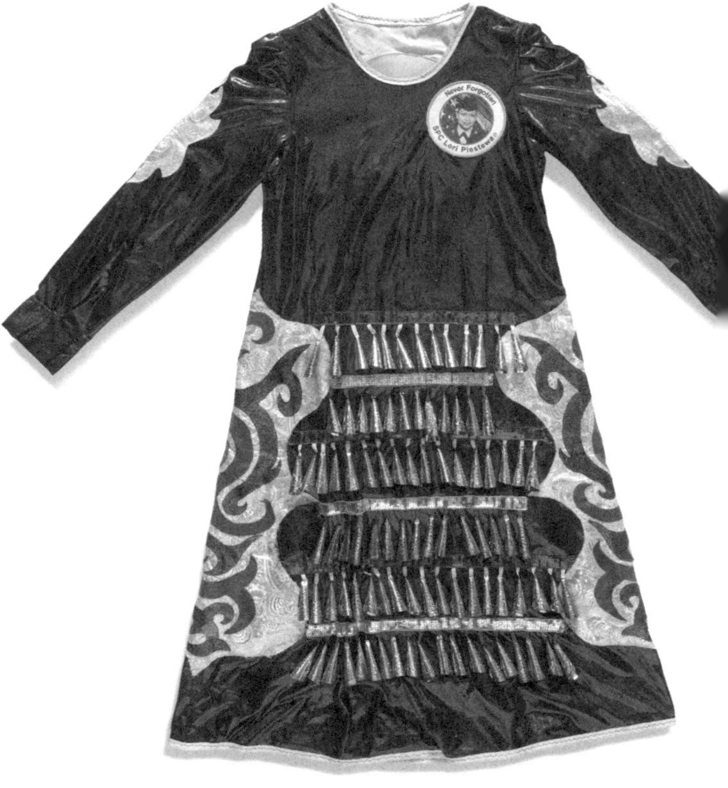
Never Forgotten
SPC Lori Piestewa

In the 2013 presidential inaugural parade, Mitchelene BigMan (Crow/Hidatsa) wore this powwow dress with military patches representing her status as a Native American woman, US Army veteran, and founding president of Native American Women Warriors.
NATIONAL MUSEUM of the AMERICAN INDIAN

Don't ever
underestimate
the impact you can have,
because history has
shown us that

COURAGE
CAN BE
CONTAGIOUS,

and hope can take on
a life of its own.

Michelle Obama, 2011

The least
I can do is

SPEAK OUT

for those
who cannot
speak for
themselves.

Jane Goodall, 1989

Giant pandas are a vulnerable species. Fewer than 2,000 pandas
thrive in their native habitat in central China, while an estimated
500 live in zoos and breeding centers around the world.
SMITHSONIAN'S NATIONAL ZOO

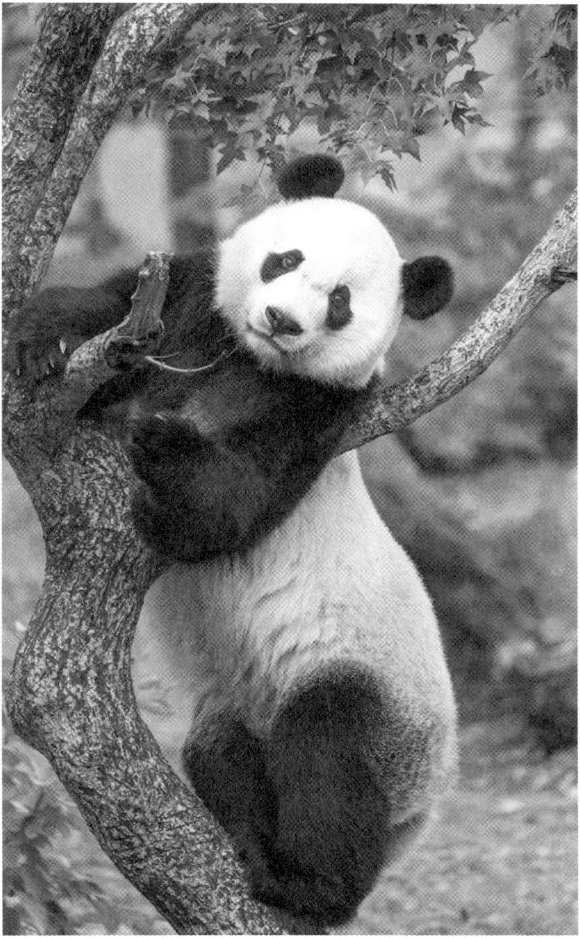

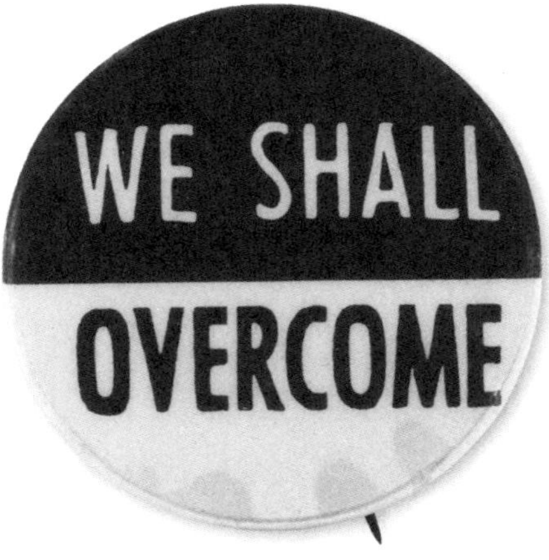
WE SHALL
OVERCOME

This button, produced in the 1960s, references the gospel song and civil rights anthem "We Shall Overcome," sung at the 1963 March on Washington.
NATIONAL MUSEUM of AFRICAN AMERICAN HISTORY and CULTURE

When you see
something that
is not right,
not just, not fair,
**you have a
moral obligation**
to say something.
To do something.

John Lewis, 2019

One of the most famous gems in the world, the Hope Diamond weighs
45.52 carats and is surrounded by 16 white diamonds.
NATIONAL MUSEUM of NATURAL HISTORY

Fashion is about dressing according to what's fashionable.

STYLE *is* MORE ABOUT BEING YOURSELF.

Oscar de la Renta, 2009

I would rather walk with a friend in the dark than walk alone in the light.

· ○ ○ ☼ ○ ○ ·

Helen Keller

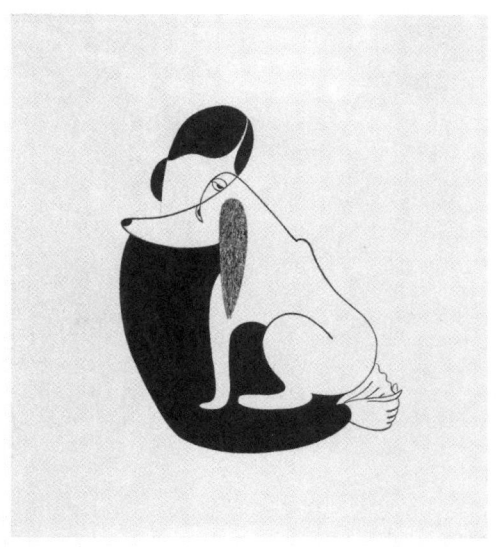

Created using a brush with black ink and white gouache, Christina Malman's drawing of a woman holding a dog appeared in the December 28, 1935, issue of the *New Yorker*.

COOPER HEWITT, SMITHSONIAN DESIGN MUSEUM

It's true that things are beautiful when they work.

ART IS FUNCTION.

Giannina Braschi, 1994

Albert Paley was a successful jeweler when he entered his iconic steel, brass, copper, and bronze sculpture *Portal Gates* into the Renwick Gallery's national competition for doors to the museum's shop.
RENWICK GALLERY, SMITHSONIAN AMERICAN ART MUSEUM

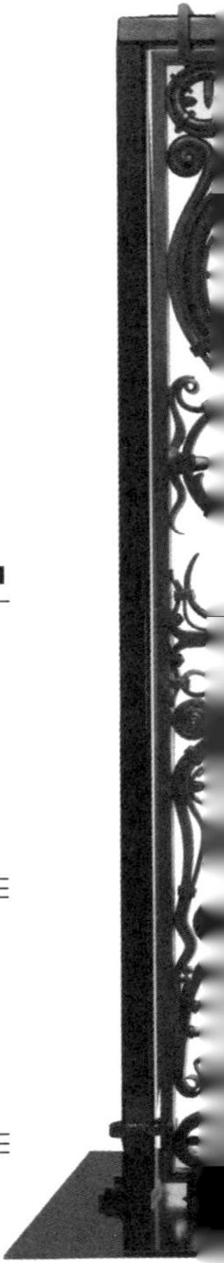

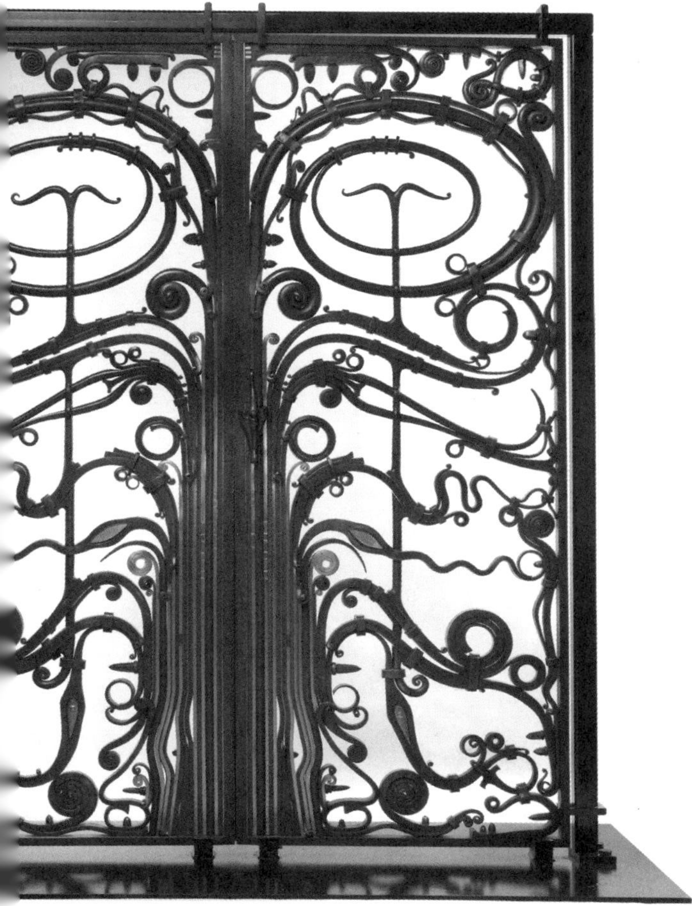

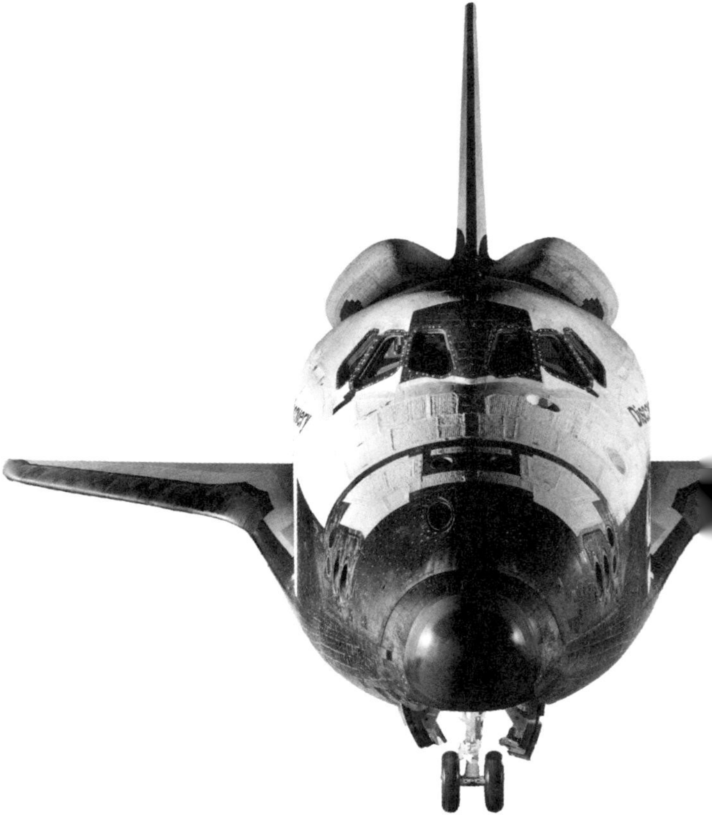
Discovery
Disco

From 1984 to 2012, *Discovery* flew 39 Earth-orbital missions, spent a total of 365 days in space, and traveled almost 150 million miles.
NATIONAL AIR and SPACE MUSEUM

*IMAGINATION
will often
carry us
to worlds that
never were.*

But
without it
we go
NOWHERE.

Carl Sagan, 1980

My work with glass transforms the notion that Native artists are only best when traditional materials are used. It has helped advocate on the behalf of all Indigenous people—

AFFIRMING THAT WE ARE STILL HERE—

and that we are declaring who we are through our art in connection to our culture.

Preston Singletary

Created by Tlingit artist Preston Singletary, *Raven Steals the Sun* represents the tribe's story about the origins of the celestial bodies, in which the trickster Raven captures the sun, moon, and stars and releases them into the world.

NATIONAL MUSEUM of the AMERICAN INDIAN

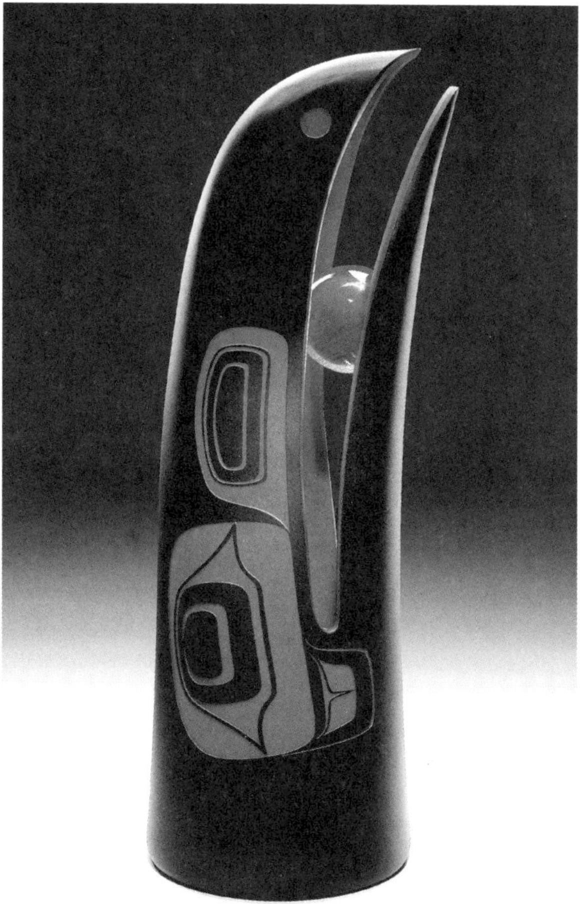

Chuck Brown, known as the "Godfather of Go-Go,"
the official music of the District of Columbia, played this
blonde Gibson ES-335 guitar throughout his career.
ANACOSTIA COMMUNITY MUSEUM

"Whatever you do
big or small,

DO IT WELL

OR DON'T

DO IT

AT ALL."

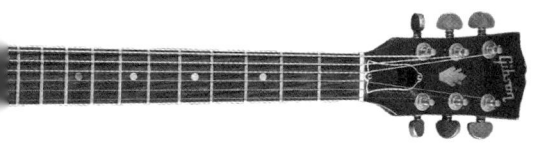

Chuck Brown

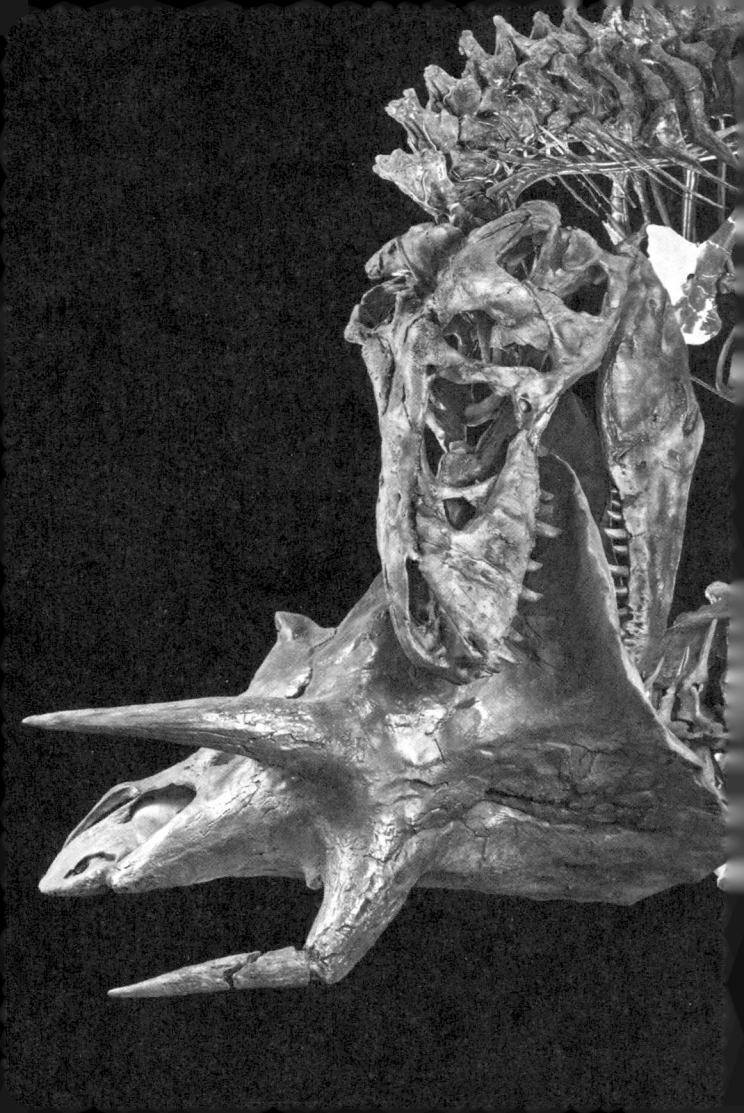

If nature teaches any lesson,

IT LOUDLY PROCLAIMS LIFE'S DIVERSITY.

◆

Stephen Jay Gould, 1983

The *Tyrannosurus rex* (known as the Nation's *T. rex*), displayed here looming over a stricken *Triceratops horridus*, was found in Montana in 1988 and was the first skeleton to preserve a nearly complete forearm.
NATIONAL MUSEUM of NATURAL HISTORY

Grown men may learn from very little children, for *the* HEARTS *of* LITTLE CHILDREN ARE PURE, and, therefore, the Great Spirit may show to them many things which older people miss.

Black Elk (Oglala Lakota)

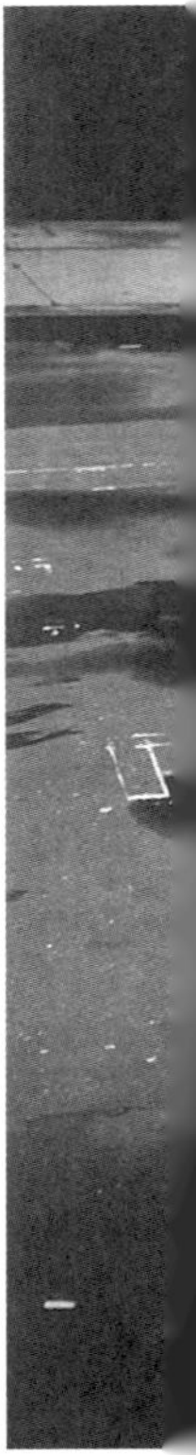

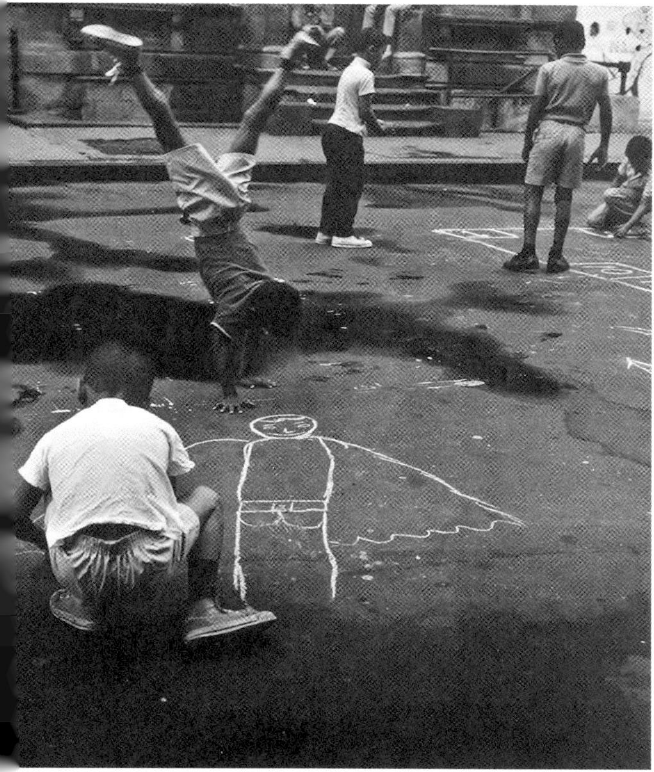

Hiram Maristany's photographs offer a rare glimpse into the bustling community of New York City's El Barrio neighborhood, including this 1965 image called *Children at Play*.

SMITHSONIAN AMERICAN ART MUSEUM

HAPPINESS

depends more
upon the internal
frame of a person's
own mind than
on the externals
in the world.

George Washington, 1787

Gilbert Stuart's monumental 1796 portrait of George Washington,
known as the Lansdowne portrait, likely depicts the president giving
his annual address to Congress in December 1795.
NATIONAL PORTRAIT GALLERY

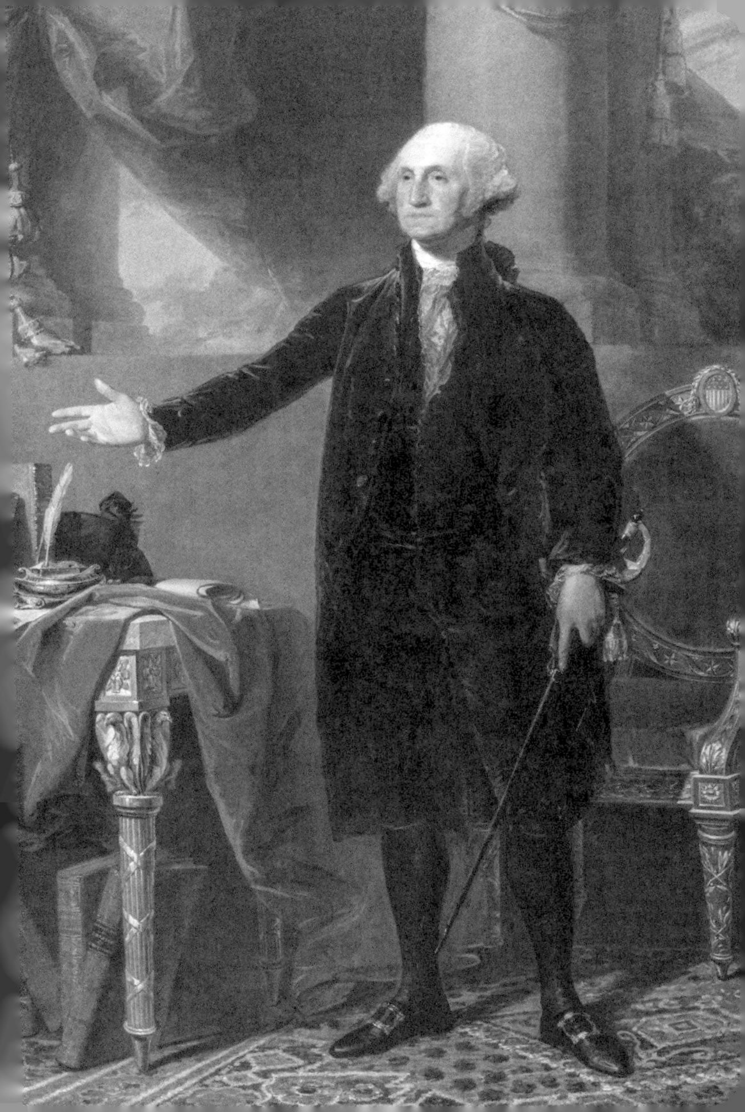

**Freedom is not
worth having
if it does
not connote**

FREEDOM

TO ERR.

Mahatma Gandhi, 1931

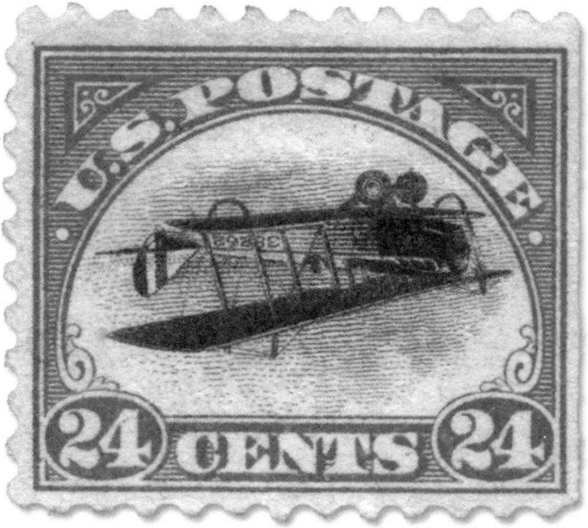
U.S. POSTAGE
24
CENTS
24

First issued on May 14, 1918, this stamp became known as the “inverted Jenny” due to its center image of the Curtiss JN-4 “Jenny” biplane being printed upside down.
NATIONAL POSTAL MUSEUM

An *ARTIST is NOT PAID for HIS LABOR*

BUT FOR HIS VISION.

James McNeill Whistler

Artist James McNeill Whistler completed *Harmony in Blue and Gold: The Peacock Room* in 1877 for English shipping magnate Frederick Leyland. In 1904 Charles Freer purchased the room and installed it in his home in Detroit, Michigan.

FREER GALLERY of ART

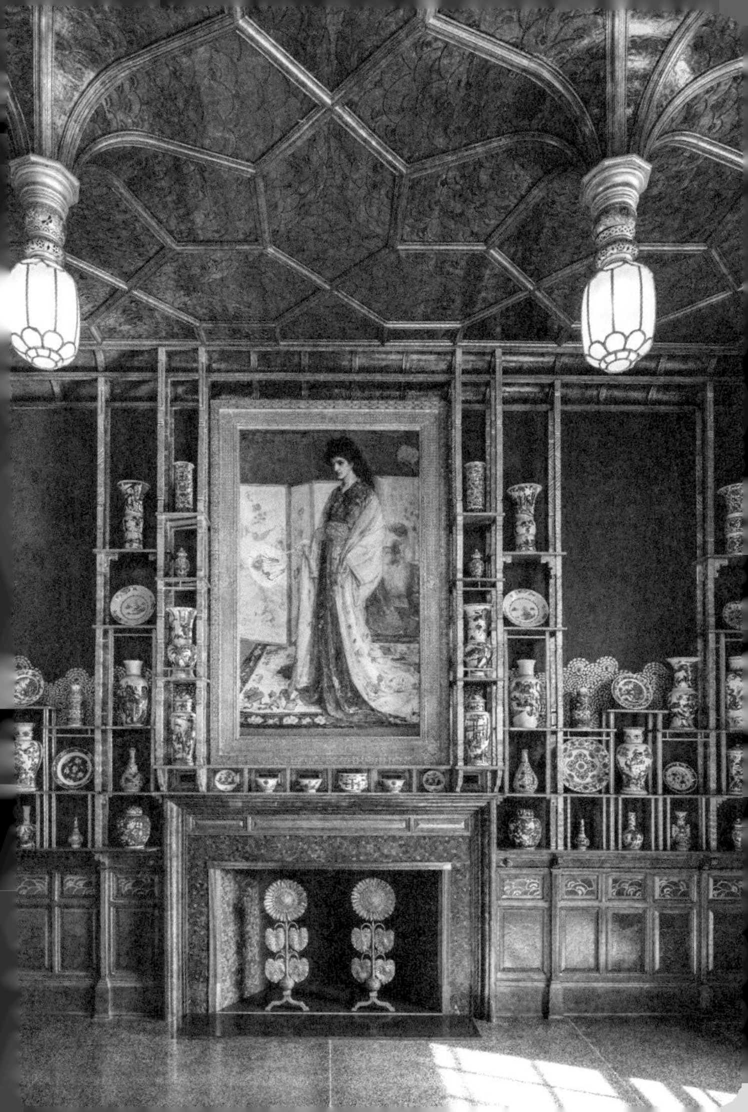

President Abraham Lincoln acquired this top hat
from J. Y. Davis, a hatmaker in Washington, DC. The last time
he put it on was to go to Ford's Theatre on April 14, 1865.

NATIONAL MUSEUM of AMERICAN HISTORY

I LEAVE YOU, *hoping that the lamp of liberty will burn in your bosoms until there shall no longer be a doubt that*

ALL MEN

ARE

CREATED

FREE

and

EQUAL.

Abraham Lincoln, 1858

Image and quotation credits

In order of appearance

Smithsonian Castle: Photo by Ken Rahaim. Quotation from the will of James Smithson. Smithsonian Castle with Buffalo: Image courtesy of the Smithsonian Institution Archives. Star-Spangled Banner: Image courtesy of the National Museum of American History. Lockheed Vega 5B: Image courtesy of the National Air and Space Museum. Gift of the Franklin Institute. Quotation by Amelia Earhart, from ameliaearhart.com. Muhammad Ali's boxing gloves: Collection of the National Museum of African American History and Culture, 2012.173.3ab. Quotation by Muhammad Ali, from espn.com. Smithsonian Institution stamp: Image courtesy of the National Postal Museum. Quotation by Albert Einstein, from a letter dated March 24, 1954. © Princeton University Press. Manhattan Bridge: Berenice Abbott, 1936, Smithsonian American Art Museum, Gift of George McNeil, 1983.16.6. Image courtesy of the Smithsonian American Art Museum. Quotation by Berenice Abbott, from "The Unflinching Eye of Berenice Abbott," ARTnews, January 1981, pp. 86-93. Ida B. Wells portrait: Image courtesy of the National Portrait Gallery. Quotation by Ida B. Wells, as quoted in The Light of Truth: Writings of an Anti-Lynching Crusader. Reduced Angled Spouted Black Piece: Magdalene Anyango N. Odundo, 1990, National Museum of African Art, 91-4-1. Image courtesy of the artist and the National Museum of African Art. Quotation by Magdalene Odundo, from ft.com. Model 302 Telephone: Image courtesy of the Cooper Hewitt, Smithsonian Design Museum. Quotation by Neil DeGrasse Tyson, from Global Ideas from Pluto's Challenger, May 21, 2009. Are Years What? (For Marianne Moore): © Mark di Suvero. Courtesy of Spacetime C.C. and Paula Cooper Gallery, New York. Image courtesy of the Hirshhorn Museum and Sculpture Garden. Quotation by Sonia Sotomayor, from npr.org. Shrine Room detail: Image courtesy of the Sackler Gallery of Art. Quotation by Tenzin Gyatso, the 14th Dalai Lama, from Kindness, Clarity, and Insight. Mitchelene BigMan's powwow dress: Image courtesy of the artist Mitchelene BigMan and the National Museum of the American Indian. Quotation by Michelle Obama, from "Remarks by the First Lady during Keynote Address at Young African Women Leaders Forum" on June 22, 2011. Panda: Image courtesy of the National Zoological Park. Quotation by Jane Goodall. We Shall Overcome button: Collection of the National Museum of African American History and Culture, Gift from Dawn Simon

Spears and Alvin Spears Sr., 2011.159.3.31. Quotation by John Lewis, from his speech on the House floor, December 18, 2019. Hope Diamond: Image courtesy of the National Museum of Natural History. Quotation by Oscar de la Renta, from the Vanity Fair article "The Importance of Being Oscar." Woman and Dog: Christina Malman, 1935. Image courtesy of the Cooper Hewitt, Smithsonian Design Museum. Quotation by Helen Keller. Portal Gates: Albert Paley, 1974, Smithsonian American Art Museum, Commissioned for the Renwick Gallery, 1975.117.1A-B. Image courtesy of the Smithsonian American Art Museum. Quotation by Giannina Braschi, Empire of Dreams, 1994. Space Shuttle Discovery: Transferred from National Aeronautics and Space Administration. Image courtesy of the National Air and Space Museum. Excerpt from COSMOS by Carl Sagan, © 1980 by Druyan-Sagan Associates, Inc.. Used by permission of Random House, an imprint and division of Penguin Random House LLC. All rights reserved. Raven Steals the Sun: Preston Singletary. Image courtesy of the artist and the National Museum of the American Indian. Quotation by Preston Singletary, from prestonsingletary.com. Chuck Brown guitar: Image courtesy of the Anacostia Community Museum. Quotation by Chuck Brown. © the Chuck Brown Estate. The Nation's T. Rex: Courtesy of the US Army Corps of Engineers, Omaha District, and The Museum of the Rockies, Montana State University. Photo courtesy of the National Museum of Natural History. Quotation by Stephen Jay Gould, from Hen's Teeth and Horse's Toes. Children at Play: Hiram Maristany, 1965, printed 2016, Smithsonian American Art Museum, Museum purchase through the Smithsonian Latino Initiatives Pool, administered by the Smithsonian Latino Center, 2016.30.7. © 1965, Hiram Maristany. Image courtesy of the artist and the Smithsonian American Art Museum. Quotation by Black Elk, from The Sacred Pipe: Black Elk's Account of the Seven Rites of the Oglala Sioux. George Washington portrait: Image courtesy of the National Portrait Gallery. Quotation by George Washington, from a letter from George Washington to Mary Ball Washington, Thursday, February 15, 1787. Inverted Jenny stamp: Image courtesy of the National Postal Museum. Quotation by Mahatma Gandhi, Right to Freedom. Peacock Room: Image courtesy of the Freer Gallery of Art. Quotation by James Whistler. Abraham Lincoln's hat: Image courtesy of the National Museum of American History. Quotation by Abraham Lincoln, from Collected Works of Abraham Lincoln, Volume 2. Speech at Chicago, Illinois, July 10, 1858. Arts and Industries Building with rockets: Image courtesy of the Smithsonian Institution Archives. Arts and Industries building: Photo by Eric Long.

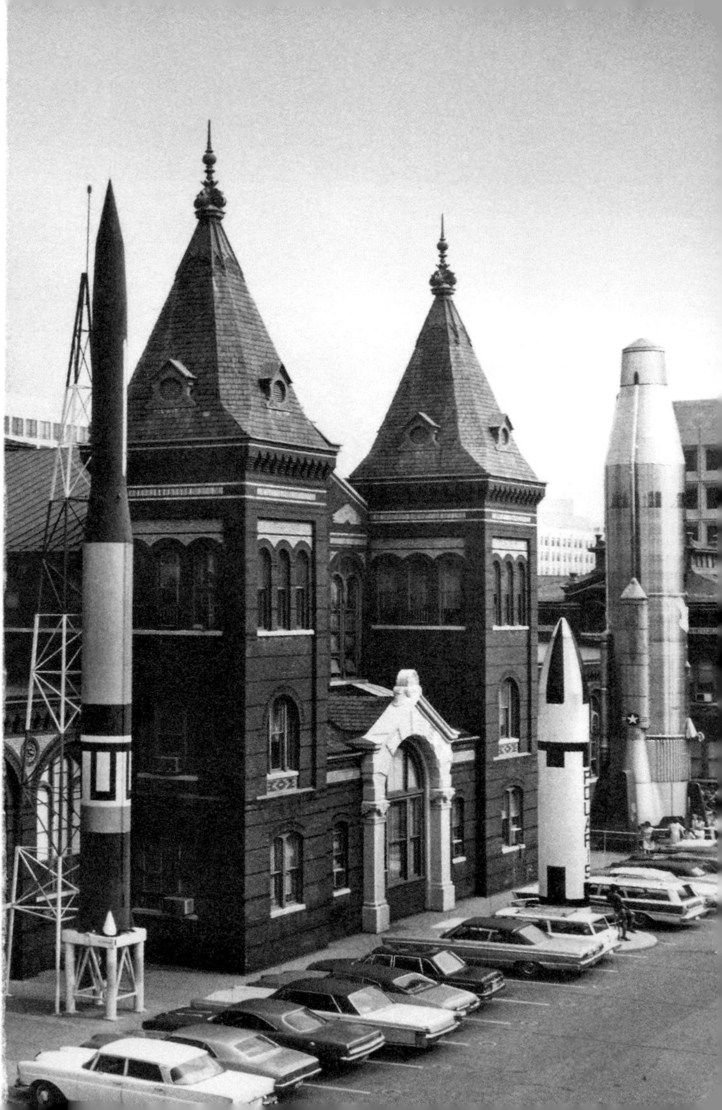

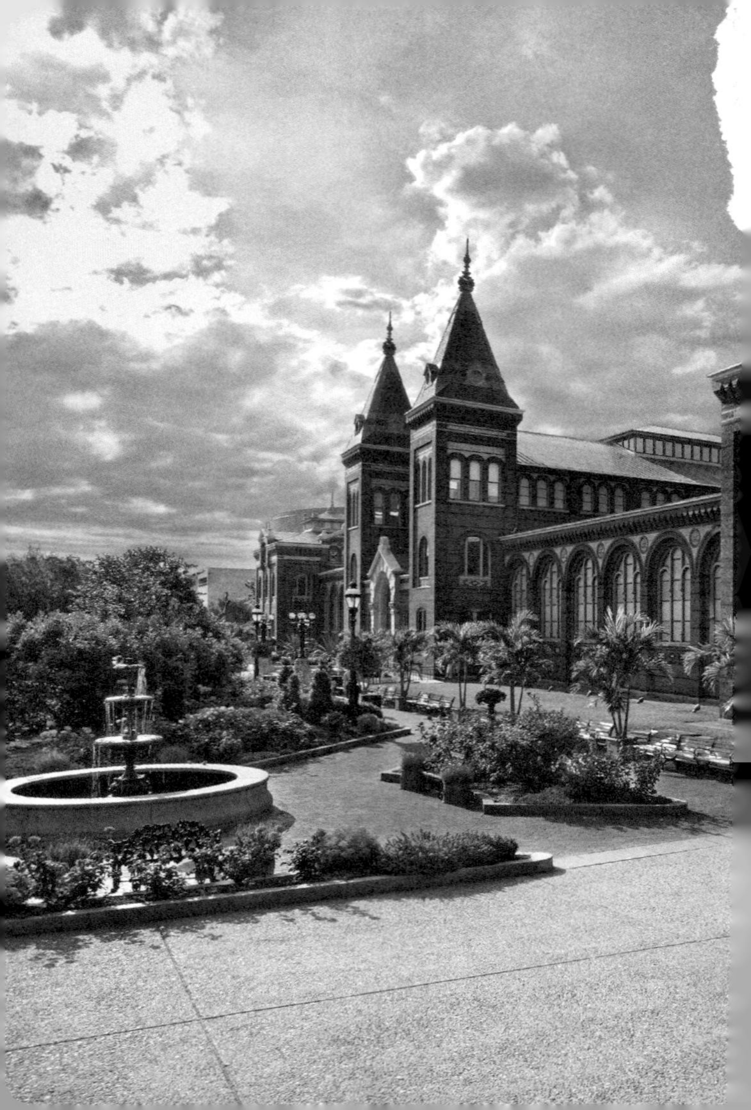